MY EVERYDAY TAGALOG WORDS

WITH NATHAN & JOHN

WRITTEN BY CARLOS CABANEROS
ILLUSTRATED BY REZA RAY

Kids of Today Inc.

New York – Manila – Toronto – Dubai – Tokyo – Riyadh – London – Paris – Beijing – Seoul – Moscow – Berlin – Rome - Singapore

KIDS OF TODAY

John is Filipino, he is from the Philippines. He immigrated to Canada at a young age. Nathan is his best friend who was born and raised in Canada. Nathan asked John if he can teach him some Tagalog words.

Aso

means

Dog

Pronunciation:

Ah-soh

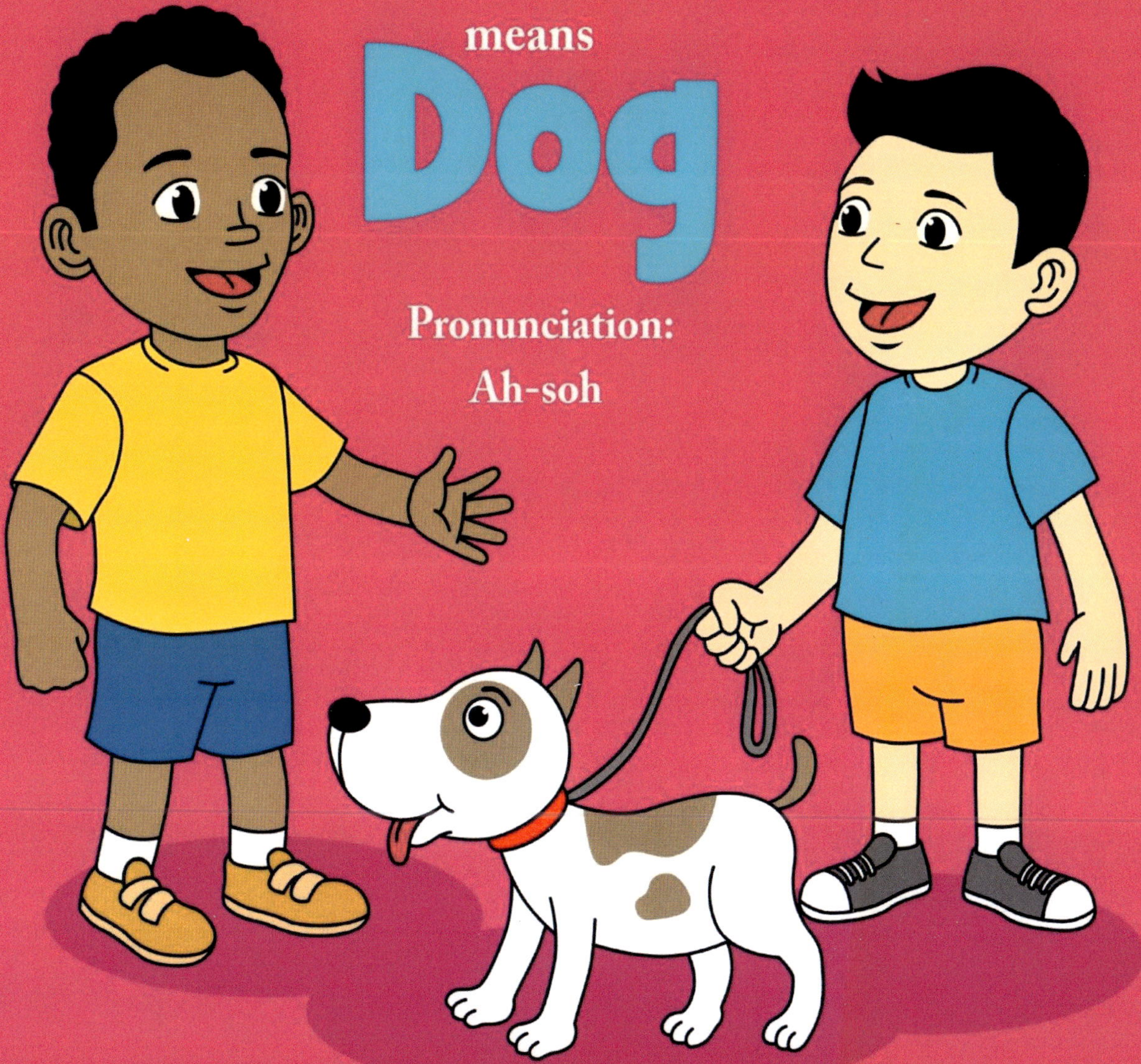

Eg. Sentence:

We love our aso, he is playful and lovable towards my family and I.

Apoy
means
Fire

Pronunciation:
Ah-poy

Eg. Sentence:
Burning wood to make us apoy to warm us in the winter cold.

Bahay means House

Pronunciation: Bah-hai

Eg. Sentence:
My bahay has different rooms, and a special room for me to play with my toys.

Baso

means

Cup

Pronunciation:

Bah-soh

Eg. Sentence:

I love to drink hot chocolate in my favourite Christmas baso.

Damit

means

Clothes

Pronunciation:

Duh-met

Eg. Sentence:

Today I am wearing my favourite damit.

Damo

means

Grass

Pronunciation:
Dah-moh

Eg. Sentence:
Damo grows in our backyard and sometimes needs trimming when it grows longer.

Eroplano

means

Airplane

Pronunciation:
Eh-roh-plano

Eg. Sentence:

I like riding on an eroplano to travel to different countries.

Elepante means Elephant

Pronunciation:
Eh-leh-pan-teh

Eg. Sentence:
An elepante is so big, I would love to see one in real life.

Gatas

means

Milk

Pronunciation:

Gah-tah-s

Eg. Sentence:

Every night before I go to sleep, I drink a glass of gatas.

Gunting

means

Scissors

Pronunciation:

Goon-ting

Eg. Sentence:

I use my gunting for my arts and crafts.

Halaman

means

Plants

Pronunciation:
Hah-lah-mah-n

Eg. Sentence:
Watering my pot of halaman every morning keeps it green and healthy.

Hagdan

means

Ladder/stairs

Pronunciation:
Hug-dan

Eg. Sentence:

I climb the hagdan with my mom to go to my room.

Ibon means Birds

Pronunciation:
Ee-Bon

Eg. Sentence:
Blue ibon, like the blue jays, fly high in the sky.

Ilong

means

Nose

Pronunciation:
ee-long

Eg. Sentence:
I use my ilong to smell all my favourite foods.

Kama

means

Bed

Pronunciation:
Kah-mah

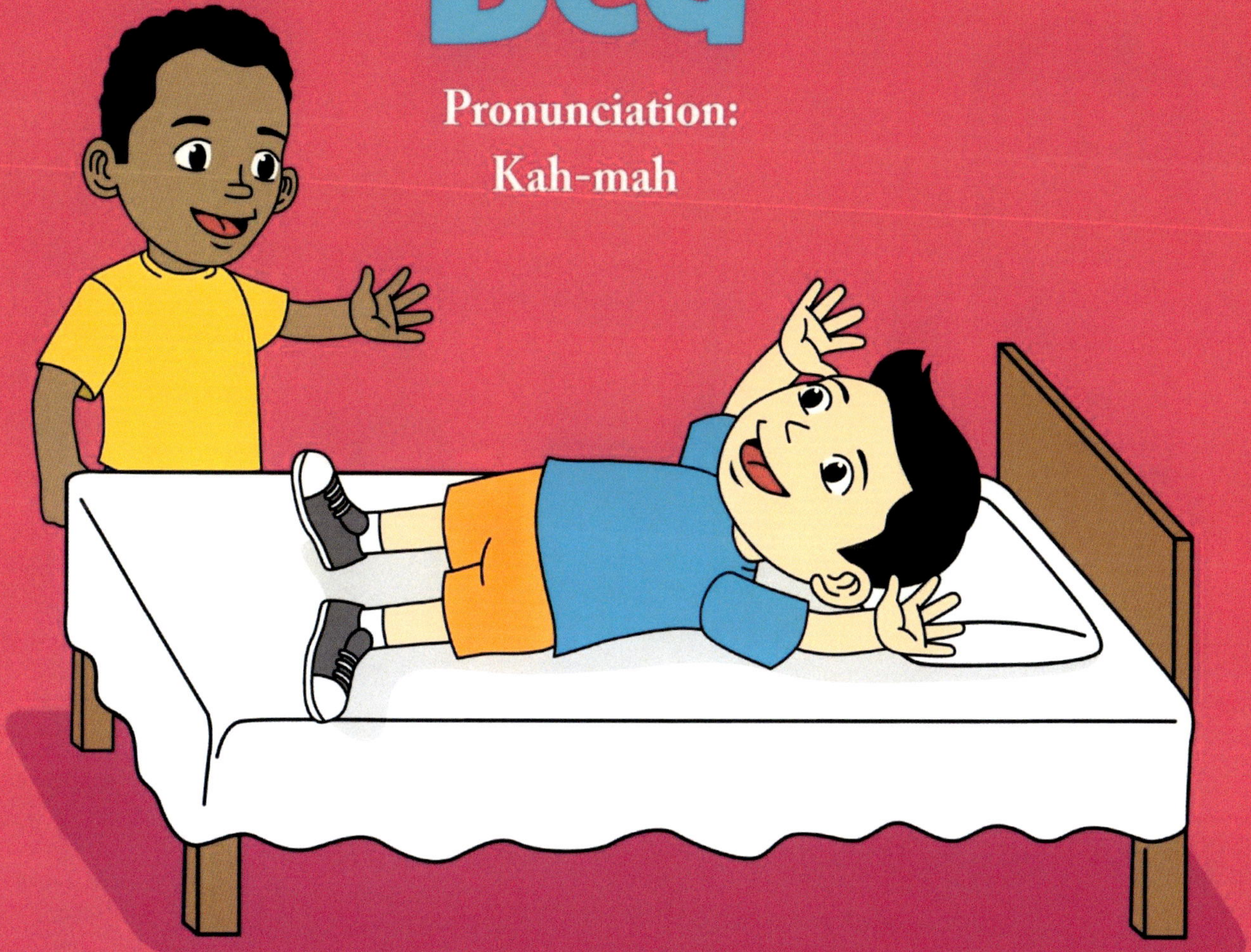

Eg. Sentence:
My Kama is soft and comfortable.

Kamiseta

means

Shirt

Pronunciation:
Kah-mih-syetah

Eg. Sentence:
I have my favourite kamiseta for going outside to play.

Lapis

means

Pencil

Pronunciation:

Lah-pis

Eg. Sentence:

I use my lapis to draw.

Lola

means

Grandmother

Pronunciation:

Loh-la

Eg. Sentence:

My lola makes the best food.

Mata

means

Eyes

Pronunciation: Mah-tah

Eg. Sentence:
We use our mata to see the beautiful world we live in.

Medyas

means

Socks

Pronunciation:
Med-yas

Eg. Sentence:
Wearing medyas keep your feet warm and comfy.

Nanay means Mother

Pronunciation:
Na-nay

Eg. Sentence:
I have the best nanay in the world.

Niyog

means

Coconut

Pronunciation:
Nee-Yog

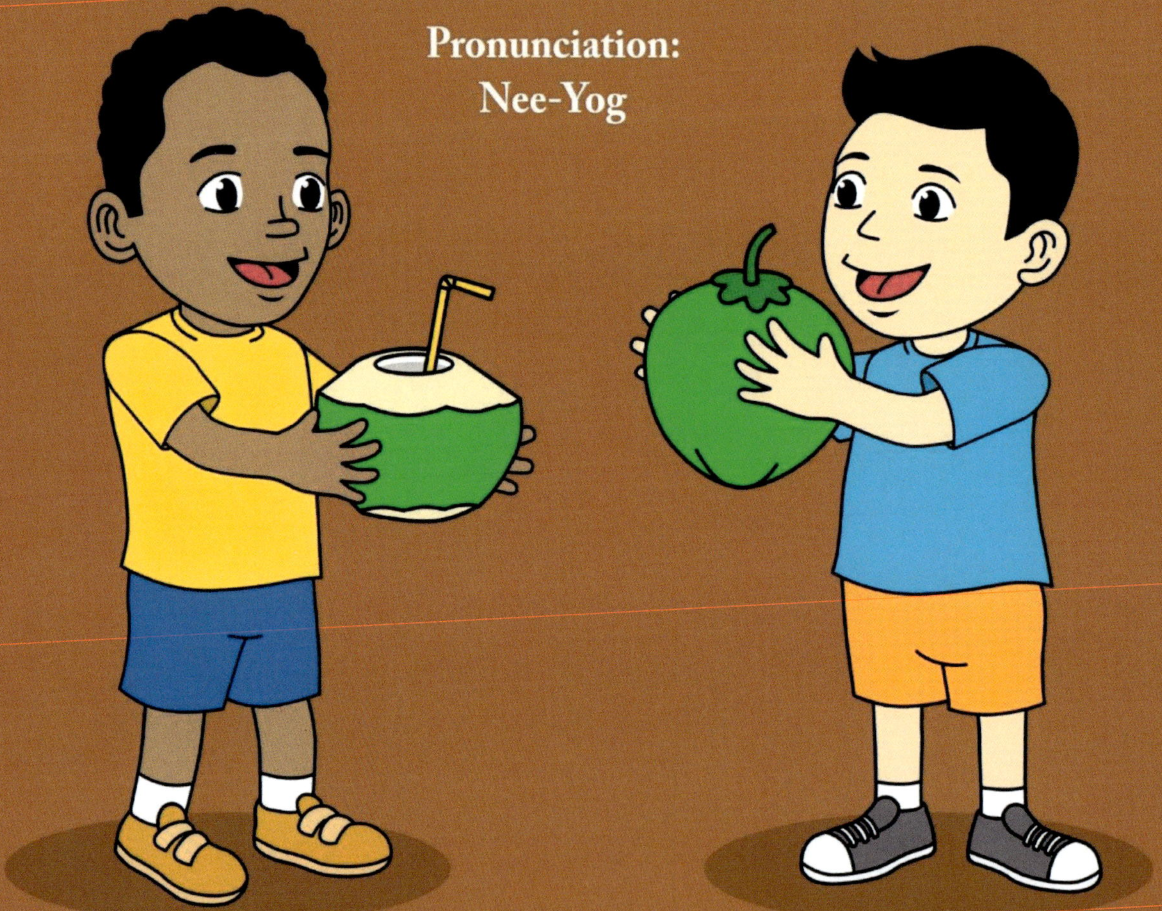

Eg. Sentence:
Niyog only grows in tropical countries. They are very delicious.

Oso means Bear

Pronunciation:
Oh-soh

Eg. Sentence:
A cute, intelligent oso has an excellent sense of smell, sight and hearing.

Oras

means

Time

Pronunciation:
Oh-rahs

Eg. Sentence:
I have to remember the oras to get to school on time.

Puno

means

Tree

Pronunciation:
Poo-noh

Eg. Sentence:
There is a big green puno at the park.

Pusa

means

Cat

Pronunciation:
Poo-sah

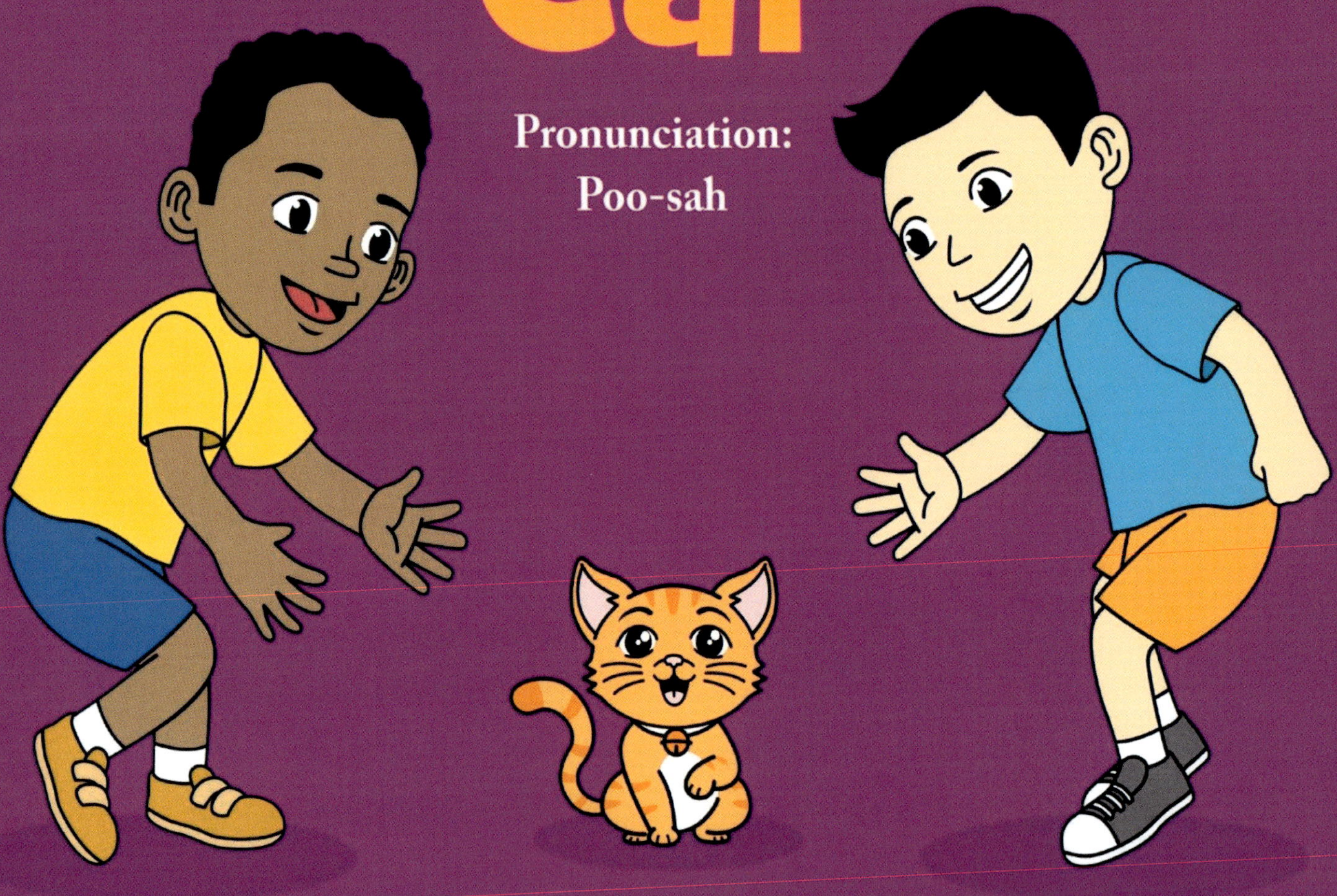

Eg. Sentence:
My pet pusa loves to sleep.

Radyo means Radio

Pronunciation:
Rad-yoh

Eg. Sentence:
I love listening to the radyo when I'm in the car.

Relo

means

Watch

Pronunciation:
Reh-loh

Eg. Sentence:
I look at my relo to see the time.

Salamin

means

Glass

Pronunciation:
Sah-lah-mean

Eg. Sentence:
While I brush my teeth, I look at myself in the salamin.

Suklay

means

Comb/hair brush

Pronunciation:

Sook-lai

Eg. Sentence:

Using my blue suklay when my hair is messy.

Tatay means Father

Pronunciation:
Tah-tahy

Eg. Sentence:
My tatay always plays fun games with me.

Telepono

means

Telephone

Pronunciation:
Te-le-poh-noh

Eg. Sentence:
I use the telepono to call my friends.

Ulap means Clouds

Pronunciation:
Ooo-lap

Eg. Sentence:
There are so many ulap in the sky today.

Ulan

means

Rain

Pronunciation:
Ooo-lahn

Eg. Sentence:
Ulan ulan go away, please don't get me wet today.

Walis

means

Broom

Pronunciation:
Wa-lis

Eg. Sentence:
I use a walis to sweep the floor.

Yeso

means

Chalk

Pronunciation:
Yeh-soh

Eg. Sentence:
Sometimes during recess my friends and I play with yeso.

Wow, I had so much fun learning all these new words in Tagalog John!
I am so happy you enjoyed them! Maybe we can do this again next time
We sure will!

kidsoftodayinc@gmail.com

Made in the USA
Coppell, TX
05 November 2026

11302979R00026